See It

by Ruth Montgomery

Photodisc/Punchstock

I see a big city!

I see a big house!

I see a big fish!

Christian Beirle González/Getty Images

Photodisc/Punchstock

I see a big hill!

I see a big tree!

A L Christensen/Getty Images

Scott Bauer - USDA Natural Resources Conservation Service

I see a big farm!